Enjoy your time
in Nature !

## What Readers Are Saying About
### *What's Under That Rock, Papa?*

"*What's Under That Rock, Papa?* by Dave Bauer is ALL a children's storybook should be! It is entertaining as well as educational, providing young children with a great story as well as important information about the world in which they live. The most compelling reason I would read this book to children is that it exudes a passion for learning! As an educator in a teacher preparation program, I will use this book in my college classroom to model the importance of student-centered inquiry learning. I hope this is only the first of 'The Bauer Family' children's books!"

> —*Nicki M. Calabrese, Ph.D., Coordinator of Early Childhood Education, Canisius College, Buffalo, NY.*

"Sometimes the best thing for young children to do is slow down and take the time to go out in their backyard or local park and start turning over rocks to see what they can find. This book encourages this behavior, and also highlights the importance of having an adult to share in these experiences."

> —*Scott Lawson, Early Childhood Programs Specialist, Buffalo Zoo*

"Dave Bauer reminds us that children are hungry for nature and relationship, and in this beautiful book he gives us both."

> —*Mary Carol Dearing, Elementary School Nature Club Advisor*

"Dave Bauer brings a close relationship with his grandchildren as well as nature exploration to this fun book that any child will relate to, especially those who have turned over a rock to examine the bugs underneath."

> —*Judith Frizlen, Director, Rose Garden, Early Childhood Center, author,* Words for Parents in Small Doses

"The pleasures of reading and exploring the natural world with curiosity and wonder shine through the pages of Dave Bauer's book for young readers."

> —*Tim Grant, Editor,* Green Teacher

# What's Under That Rock, Papa?

Written by Dave Bauer
Illustrated by Tia Canonico

 Brandylane Publishers, Inc.
WWW.BRANDYLANEPUBLISHERS.COM

ISBN: 978-1-9399306-6-8

Library of Congress Control Number: 978-1-9399306-6-8

Printed in the United States

Published by

Brandylane Publishers, Inc.
WWW.BRANDYLANEPUBLISHERS.COM

To Serea and Kai for reawakening in
me the wonder found in nature.
And to my daughter, Jessica,
for helping the seeds of curiosity
to grow in her children.

Dear Reader,

My wife and I experience wonderful insights when we spend time with our two grandchildren, Serea and Kai. I love to see their excitement when they run to the book basket in our home and call out, "Grammy, read me this book!" Serea and Kai snuggle close to their grandmother as she reads aloud to them. This shared reading experience is truly special, allowing them to explore the exciting world each new book offers.

I find sharing moments in nature with these children, especially in areas I call "everyday places," like backyards and areas close-by in my community, to be a fascinating experience. Children's wonder and natural curiosity to discover and seek understanding are gifts they give freely.

I invite you to enter into these moments of discovery with an attitude of joy as you see a world unfold through Serea and Kai's eyes. I find as I assume a sense of stillness while outside with Serea and Kai, I am privileged to be guided into their world of nature.

My hope is that you and the child with whom you share this book will enjoy the fascinating journey that awaits you.

Dave Bauer

S erea and Kai are very excited! They are heading to Grammy and Papa's home for a sleepover. Their mom is coming too. Serea and Kai love these visits because they always spend so much time in nature— time filled with adventures and surprises.

Their grandfather, Papa, is a science teacher and loves nature. He can explain things that Serea and Kai don't understand. Their grandmother, Grammy, is a social worker and likes to help people. She reads them wonderful books.

On this visit, Serea and Kai's adventure begins in Grammy and Papa's backyard. It's almost sunset, and Papa is telling them a story about three children wandering into a big pine forest.

"When the skies darken and the wind gets fast and cold, the three children become nervous and scared," Papa says. Just then, Serea looks up and notices a big dark cloud above them.

"Oh, Papa, look at that huge black cloud!" Serea says, pointing. "Why are some clouds so dark?"

Papa answers, "Those clouds look dark because they are filled with raindrops, so the sunlight can't shine through them. It means a storm is coming. Let's go inside."

Papa is right: a storm does come. It comes after Serea and Kai have gone to bed. The branches outside move like witches flying past Serea's bedroom window! Bolts of lightning flash onto the walls in her room. Blasts of thunder shake her bed and rattle her windows. Serea feels scared.

Now the thunder cracks even louder, and the curtains blow wildly like ghosts. Serea's mom comes in, hugs her gently, and tells her that the angels are having fun bowling up in heaven. Serea knows from Papa that the cracking noise is actually the sound lightning makes when it heats up the air around it very quickly. Her mom's story of the angels does help her feel less nervous.

When Serea peeks out her window the next morning, she can't believe her eyes! The morning sunlight sparkles on the wet leaves and grass. She wonders, "How can things be SO calm and beautiful after such a dark, scary storm?"

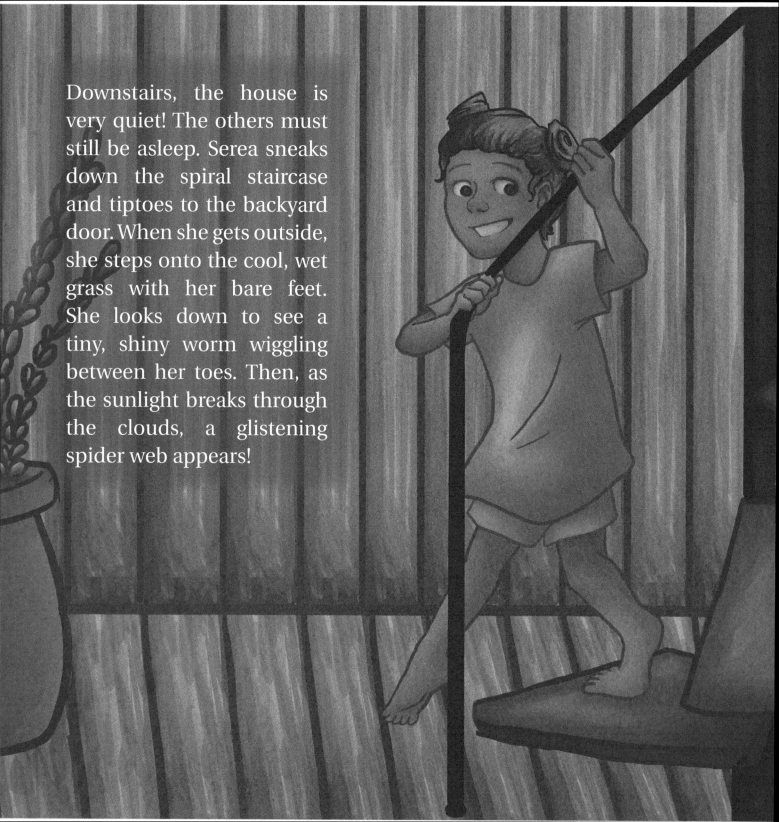

Downstairs, the house is very quiet! The others must still be asleep. Serea sneaks down the spiral staircase and tiptoes to the backyard door. When she gets outside, she steps onto the cool, wet grass with her bare feet. She looks down to see a tiny, shiny worm wiggling between her toes. Then, as the sunlight breaks through the clouds, a glistening spider web appears!

Clear, tiny water droplets have condensed on the web during the cool night. Suddenly, a powdery white moth flies into the web and gets stuck! Fast as lightning, a blue spider dances across the wet strands. Just as Serea reaches out to touch the moth, her mom calls, "Serea, can you come in here? Kai and I need help in the kitchen."

Kai asks, "Can I help make the pancakes?"

Mom says, "I have a special ingredient for these pancakes!" She opens a little container and holds it out to them. "This morning we're having worm pancakes!"

Kai and Serea reach in and touch what's inside the container. Serea's fingers brush something dry and dusty. She thinks of the wet, wriggling worm she saw moments ago. "Mom," she exclaims, "these worms are dead!"

Mom says, "Of course! They are from Papa's dried worm collection. After it rains, Papa gathers them up. They have lots of protein. Try one – they're crunchy!" Just as Serea and Kai begin to take their first bite, Mom whispers to them, "They're really chow mein noodles."

After breakfast, Mom, Kai, and Serea walk to the park. They find a quiet place to sit peacefully. Mom says this is a good way to start the day because Serea and Kai have LOTS of energy. Sitting in nature and slowing down their breathing helps them to relax. When Serea sits in nature, she feels calm and safe. Sometimes stories happen in her head.

When they return to Grammy and Papa's, Serea notices that the tall blue fountain in their yard has lots of visitors today! Little bright yellow goldfinches sweep past Kai and Serea to get drinks of water. The birds love to hop into the water and make BIG splashes.

Serea asks Papa, "Is this a way for the birds to take a bath?" Papa nods and explains that bathing helps the birds keep their feathers healthy so they can fly well.

When Kai and Serea look down into the water in the big bottom pool, they see tiny wiggly critters all about. Papa explains that they are baby mosquitoes: "Those are how mosquitoes begin their lives. They're called mosquito larvae." Kai plucks a worm from the grass and tries to put it in the water with the larvae, but Papa stops him. He says worms need air to breathe.

Serea looks around and notices some big, flat pieces of rock covering the ground near the fountain. She points to the one nearest them. "What's under that rock, Papa?"

Papa smiles. "Let's find out!"

It takes Kai and Serea working together to lift the rock. Underneath there's no grass. Instead there's dark, damp soil, and a whole zoo of tiny, crawly, squirming animals. "WOW!" says Kai. "Let me touch them!"

Kai gently catches a red wiggly worm and giggles as he holds it in his palm. He says happily, "He's tickling me, Serea!"

Kai and Serea take turns gently catching and holding the creatures they find under the rock. Then they decide to build tiny houses for them with grass and sticks, and flowers so it's pretty. One of the creatures has LOTS of legs and can scoot really fast. Papa says his name is Centipede.

After a while, they put the rock back so the creatures can rest. But Serea and Kai aren't tired. "Can we go to the park?" Serea asks. Grammy and Papa both agree to come! Serea and Kai quickly ride their scooters to each corner of the sidewalk. At the park, Kai jumps on the swing, and when he sees the crows swooping overhead, he calls out, "Caw, caw, caw!" One crow comes close and caws right back. Can the crow and Kai be talking to each other? Serea wonders.

Near the park is a winding creek with noisy geese splashing in the water. Today the water is very clear. Kai gets down on his belly and slowly crawls close to the edge of the creek. He stays still and doesn't even move a little bit. The fish get curious and come really close to his face.

Kai never even notices the big furry raccoon fishing just a little bit downstream, but the others do! Papa, Grammy, and Serea whisper quietly to each other so they don't scare the raccoon away.

Kai and Serea notice lots of litter near the woods by the creek. Grammy and Papa see it too, and Grammy says, "Let's go home and get some big bags to clean this place up!" So they do. Serea and Kai are amazed at all the trash they can find in the woods, just by looking down around their feet. Papa tells them, "Litter is 'lost sunlight.' All the litter started out long ago as energy from the sun!"

When they get back to the house, they stash the bags of litter in the outdoor trash can, and place some of the items in the recycling bin. Mom and Grammy start to make lunch. Meanwhile, Papa, Kai, and Serea carry a small metal pail full of food scraps from the kitchen, and dump it into one of the compost bins in the backyard. Serea looks into the compost bin and says, "Wow! There are LOTS of tiny creatures living in the compost!"

Papa explains that those creatures, and especially the worms, are eating the kitchen scraps and making fresh soil. Papa says that when Serea and Kai come back to visit again, they can help him spread the finished compost into the flowerbeds in the yard.

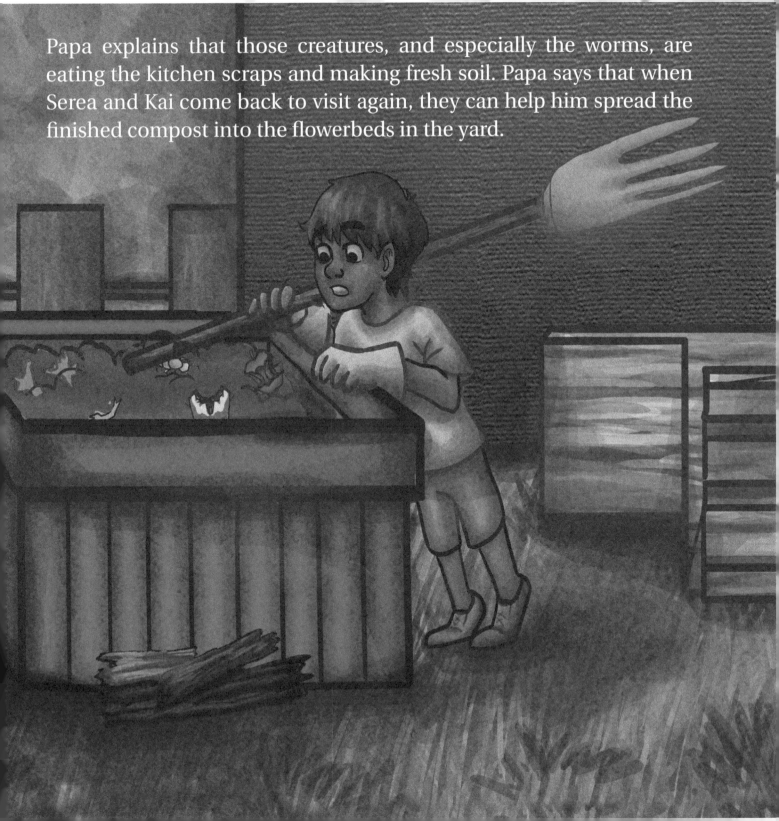

While Kai and Serea eat their lunch at the picnic table in the backyard, they spot a big, fat toad moving under the back porch! Serea peeks under the porch and sees it hiding in the shade. She says, "Kai, crawl under there and see if you can get it!"

Just as Kai begins to crawl into the dark shadows, the toad hops right out in front of Serea, and she picks it up gently in her hands.

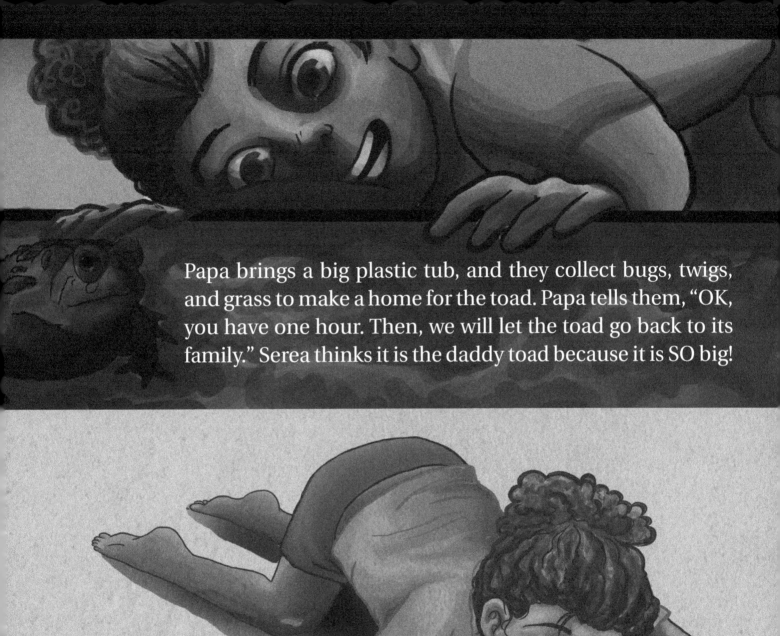

Papa brings a big plastic tub, and they collect bugs, twigs, and grass to make a home for the toad. Papa tells them, "OK, you have one hour. Then, we will let the toad go back to its family." Serea thinks it is the daddy toad because it is SO big!

The afternoon is warm and sunny, so Grammy, Kai, and Serea snuggle up to read a book on the bench in the backyard. They sit in the shade of the big maple tree. In this story, Grammy reads about a family who had to walk a long way to get water. Grammy says, "In many places in the world, people can't just turn on a faucet to get water. That's why we need to be sure to turn off our faucets. We all have to do our part." Grammy often tells them they can help change the world and make it better.

With the sun shining so brightly, Papa gets Kai a container of water and an old paintbrush. He says, "Kai, see if you can paint me a long snake on the blacktop driveway." But the snake keeps disappearing before Kai can finish putting the eyes on the snake's head! Papa says, "This is called evaporation. The sun's energy heats up the water, and it disappears into the air. Way up in the sky, the water cools off, and this helps to make clouds appear. Then the water comes back down as rain."

Later that night, just after Kai and Serea get into their pajamas, Serea spots some tiny specks of light in the darkness of the backyard.

"Kai!" she says. "Let's go outside and see!" In the air by the hedge, the light specks appear for a few seconds, move a few feet, and then suddenly disappear! Kai and Serea sit very still near the hedge, hoping to get close to the specks of light.

"What are they?" Kai asks.

Serea remembers what Papa told her on their last visit. "They're fireflies," she says. She reaches out her hand as one flies past. "Oh, Kai," she says. "What a perfect end to a perfect day!"

Just like Serea and Kai, you too can have adventures and find hidden treasures in your backyard and the places you visit. An amazing world is right outside for you to explore, so go outdoors and see where the wonders of nature will lead you!

Here's a short list of fun things you can do in nature. Try to add a few of your own before you close the book today!

- Visit a creek near your house. See what kind of wildlife you can spot beneath the water's surface.

- Lift up some big stones or roll over an old log in your yard. There's really cool stuff in the damp, dark dirt.

- Make "worm pancakes" or another creation inspired by nature.

- Look for hidden spider webs in the early morning when there's lots of dew on the grass.

- Look for fireflies in your backyard before you go to bed.

- Try to catch a frog or toad – be gentle and put it back in nature soon.

- Set up a compost bin in your yard – you'll see LOTS of worms in a few weeks! Find out how at www.whatsunderthatrockpapa.com

- What's your idea or adventure???

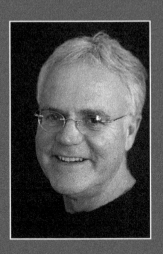

## About the Author

Dave Bauer loves the outdoors, hiking, biking and cross-country skiing. In addition to teaching environmental science for thirty-four years, he is a sustainability and environmental consultant, leadership trainer and business facilitator with his company, Sustainable Earth Solutions. He lives in Buffalo, New York. This is Dave's first book.

## About the Illustrator

Tia Canonico is a recent graduate of Rochester Institute of Technology and has been drawing for as long as she can remember. She keeps herself well rounded in the realm of entertainment and storytelling as an artist of many trades. In her spare time she finds inspiration in books, movies, video games and nature, and she also draws motivation from within herself. She is currently freelancing on Long Island, New York.

CPSIA information can be obtained
at www.ICGtesting.com
Printed in the USA
BVHW05*2317211018
529957BV00002B/2/P

9 781939 930668